Somewhere Here & Now

Zsofia Bertrand

BookLeaf
Publishing

Presentation by *BookLeaf Publishing*

Web: www.bookleafpub.com

E-mail: info@bookleafpub.com

ISBN: 9789357441445

First edition 2023

ACKNOWLEDGEMENT

All the endless love I've received from the dawn of my existence to now deserves acknowledging.

PREFACE

You all exist within versions of the words I write. I love you all. I honor your presence in this inspiration.

Wisdom

I am for certain that I am uncertain.

Mamcsi

I am a blank canvas
Reborn every day
As if I had just first entered my
Mothers loving embrace

Breathe

Bewildered I am to know all but nothing.
I believe I have no way to explain it in its
beauty.
The putrid beauty of it all.

Exotic smells of the universe.

A fragrant blend of
Aspirations
Bewonderment
Delicate longing
Incessant pleading

Soft riffs
Whiffs
    The small tickle in your throat
You know the one?

#4

And in these times-
recall on the severity of the past.
Relinquish the emphasis
of the future.
Allow the stimulation of the present
to release your suffering.
The decadence of this time is minute
in the vast ocean of existence.
The repercussions serve their time
As they do their lack thereof.
Here and now there is everything
In and out of itself.
Surrounding the truth
The reality of senselessness
No boundaries
No heaviness
Strictly understanding
Strictly embracing
Ever observing
Truth

Peaceful pain

I try so hard to piece the puzzle
To align the way the things that are

Yet I always come to a block
A wall
That stands too tall

The reality of the peaceful pain

The ruptured torture of rise/fall

From These we Heal.

6

At this point, you live in my subconscious like a
blooming cactus in the desert- unwatered for
months but still gorgeous as ever- growing with
the heat of the sun and blooming with the moon.

FTWH- Ocean.

Your love was like a raging river
Blocked by a dam
You built yourself.
I don't blame you.
Knowing where your rivers been,
I would have done the same
But you deserve to be free and united with the
blissful ocean
It awaits you with open arms
If you only let her.
But know that becoming one with the ocean
doesn't mean losing yourself
It means being even greater than the rivers past.
The fear of losing yourself has holed you behind
your walls
Walls of which I see beyond.
Oceans can be unpredictable,
As is everything else.
I choose to be serene then wild
Depending on what form needs fixing
Being unpredictable with the currents of life has
taught me far greater things than a dam ever
would.

FTWH- part of u

I take with me
a piece of you
Your love instilled
In my world view
Your thoughts and dreams
Part of the new
New way I see
This self of truth
Such ways I've grown
That capture you
Flowing still
To my next move
I love you still
I thank you too
For making me
A part of you.

Whole/Healed

I hate to admit it, but that's just the kind of love
I'm looking for.
Deeply devoted, borderline blind.
So lost in the fire, the burn my new home.

Now it's all embers of what was.
The scars once visible- now fully healed over.

Fear sometimes envelops me.
The thought 'maybe never again'
Haunts me.

But I'm slowly coming to befriend the truth that
Never Again is hope.
Hope that I can feel-
Just not like that, at least.

I try the new lens on for feel.
I don't want wild anymore.
I want safe, I want found.

Caressing, flowing.

The way of the water, reaching even the darkest
crevices.

The ones I didn't even know still sizzle.

I'll always be reminded of that love
The heat. Rapid, uncontrollable. Destructive but
necessary.

I hope one day I'll be loved like I love.
But until that time comes
I let Myself flow through me
Accepting all I have to offer as the healer and
the one in need of healing.

Whole nonetheless

Memories

You tell me
and you show me

The years that've flown by.

Denial and acceptance
Both circle around in my mind

The youth on our faces
The love that has graced us

Reminiscing sure does heal

0110#11

The reason I crave more
Is a simple ode
    To all my abilities.

Understand 'I am'
Is what triggers these conceurrences.

Or is that a simple truth of my human fallacies.

Perceive

We crave permanence;
yet all we have is change.
Attachment and distractions
From the one true saving grace-
Eternal shift.

Along

Do I want love again?
Or do I just want touch again?

Or do I want to grow alongside
Someone else's trust again?

To flow with someone else's
Upward trend?

*here

With strong minds
But even stronger hearts
The peace within
Creates the stars
Release yourself
Find your true calling
Societies spell
Will soon be falling
Time is here
For now and always
Keep on seeking
Through your souls hallways
The answers unclear
Or is that perception?
Our minds could be
The biggest deception.
Find yourself
In moments of bondage
Release the thoughts
Of your past knowledge
We hold the key
To our own demise
So let us prevail
Till we all suffice
A light so clear

Ahead for all
Will soon be coming
Answer the call
Listen close
To your intentions
Hone clearly on
Your souls ascension
Allow yourself
The freedom of choice
Are you a slave
Let's hear your voice.

Applause {a pause}

What I feel when I am outside
Marveling at Gods (my) creation
Lacks the ability to be confined in word

It deserves much higher praise

The praise of awareness in the simplest act
Of existence.

Simply living in it

In awe
And with disbelief
That you
That I
Am so fortunate
To be
Here
And also
Now

Against

I don't know lately
To be honest I've been feelin kind of hazy
My minds been running itself in circles
Yet I'm always finding my way over hurdlers.
I know I'm my own production of self
conceived misery
And I'm slowly shedding my past self of all
those silly commodities
My sole reminder of persistence is the simple
fact of your existence
My past my present and my future constantly
remind me to mend my sutures

You're on the sidelines cheering me on
But I would hope so because It's your own race
after all
Flowing out of me are the words of soul
Yet I didn't one day just wake up bold.
Time takes patience, even if time ain't real
Even if it's make believe, you can't force
yourself to heal.

This race I'm running is a solo endeavor
All this heavy breathing has made me more
clever

The only thing to beat is me. My competitor is
not my worst enemy.
I'm so close to the finish line, I can clearly taste
the divine
Countless hours of grueling will receive their
virtue.

It's never been about the end, for that always
shifts
It's always been about the send, pushing till it
clicks.
I choose to choose me in this race that I'm
winning
Because this minor choice is just the beginning.

Montezuma Falls.

To say I am full of pride would be an injustice of
all that I encompass here and now.
As the spray of young Gaia mists my being, I
embrace every version of myself I hold. All the
shapes in which my soul makes home.
Now,
Then,
And onward.

What a busy place
As serene as ever.
Calm and tethered.
here now
    forever.

1114

The final sip
The final bite

What have we here?
Such sweet delight.

And onward now...
No going back

The skies have cleared
[this right here is where I'm at]

6:31 am

Where do you see yourself in the next five
years?
  She asks him
As she envisions a future.
            With him?
                Without?
She doesn't know.
        She, herself, barely has the slightest clue
the answer to this question.

        But what she does know
  (And boy
        Does she know it well.)
  Is that her future is bright.

The simple details matter none.
She knows in her heart

The truth of it all.
That no matter where she is

        There

        She

        Was

?

I deserve to give myself trust.
In fact,
I feel it's owed (ode)
        Kindly.
To embrace whatever wind I may choose to
entangle my fingers with.
        What ray of sun I choose to caress on my skin

Being

We begin to waltz around with our words,
dancing (fluttering even) through the universe.
Drinking each letter in.
In a haste,
letting the tea burn.

Pouring from one cup to another.
While we glide through endless stories and
questions begging to be answered.

Fast paced, elegant, hot
    then slow.
It's the timing of the syllables from your lips that
keeps my body in Rhythm.

As the steam rises from my glass,
    pressing for more truth of the steps you
move inside your mind,
 I let you lead.
Hand pressed behind my back, first left than
right.
Stirring the contents inside the chalice of
movements and thoughts.

Moving, gathering.
Slowly assessing the unfolding of flavors.

The trickle of sweat on your upper lip tastes of
aromatic jasmine.
Speaking in tongues, our fervent flamenco
dance.
A delicate blend
A medley.
Of sounds in words
Of taste in herbs
Of sights in souls
Of touching skin
Of smells in a future becoming.
Beckoning.

The art of tea leaves
And of the merengue
Are Not often compared
    {Not enough if you ask me}
But the intricate blend of culture, generations of
wisdom and fate-
the culmination of DNA they both posses.
It's bound to meet somewhere.
Somewhere so docile.
Somewhere so raw.

Somewhere where our words no longer have
meaning. Where they had yet not gotten the
chance.
In the beginning of time.
where all but energy exists.